Genealogy for the Beginner

A PeeperPub2013

Sample the world of Genealogy and researching your family history before investing a lot of money and time.

CONTENTS

BASIC TOOLS FOR GENEALOGY

Laptop computer (optional)

Genealogy software (optional)

Digital camera/extra batteries (optional)

Loose-leaf notebook (3-ring binder)

Notepads (legal size works well)

Pencils (regular and colored)

Pencil sharpener (hand held)

Eraser

Pens (regular and colored-some archives and libraries may not allow pens)

Post-it notes-some archives and libraries may not allow post-it notes or other such page markers

Scrap paper cut in strips to mark pages

Hand held magnifying glass

Change for copiers and parking meters

Paper punch

Hole reinforcements

Paper clips

Copies of research (LEAVE ORIGINALS AT HOME)

- Surname list (alphabetical list of names you are searching in the area
- Research log
- Family Group Sheets (bring extra blank sheets as well as those you are working on)
- Pedigree charts (bring extra blank sheets as well as those you are working on)
- Blank preprinted census forms

Library and archive information (location, hours)

Map of area visiting

Photo ID

Band-Aids (in case of paper cuts)

COMMONLY USED TERMS

If you are new to genealogy there are a few basic terms you should know to help during your search. Knowing and understanding these terms will help your search progress more accurately and quickly. Genealogy can be time consuming and it is disappointing when you find you have followed the wrong leads. Looking for, and following the proper branches of your family tree will make the fruits of your labor that much sweeter.

- Ancestor-person or people from whom one is descended. A relative.

- Biography-a narrative of important events of a person's life.

- Census-list of inhabitants of a certain area or region, done on a federal or state basis.

- Death notice-a short mention of a person's death, usually in a newspaper. Shorter than an obituary.

- Deed-a legal document conveying real property.

- Descendant-a person who descends from an ancestor.

- Emigration-moving from one country to another or one area to another.

- Estate-property owned by a person at their time of death.

- Executor-person named in a will to handle the deceased estate.

- Extract-to copy a record or portions of it, verbatim(word for word)

- Family group sheet-a standard chart used to record the genealogical information pertaining to one family.

- Generation-all the progeny that are at the same state of descent of a common ancestor.

- Head of household-person whose name appears first in the census record of a household. Generally male if husband or father is living.

- Immigration-the act of moving into one country from another to establish a residence.

- Issue-children of a couple.

- Naturalization records-documents that are produced when an immigrant becomes a citizen of the United States.

- Obituary-a detailed announcement of a person's death that lists biographical data, surviving relatives, religion and burial information.

- Original source-the original form of a historical document.

- Pedigree-one's lineage or ancestry.

- Pedigree chart-chart used to record detailed genealogical information.

- Plat-a map showing details of who owns property. Often used in cemeteries to show locations of graves. Some small towns also publish plat books.

- Primary source-a record created at the time of an event by someone with personal knowledge of the even.

- Secondary source-a record created long after the original event; not as reliable as a primary source.

- Surname-family name or last name.

- Tax record-list of people paying taxes in a given area and their property; usually compiled on a county level every year.

- Vital records-legal records of births, deaths, marriages and divorces.

- Will-a legal document explaining the desired disposition of a person's property upon their death.

HOW TO ORGANIZE GENEALOGY INFORMATION

The advent of computers and the Internet has made the hobby of genealogy, or tracing one's ancestry, easier, faster and more organized. Computers are wonderful--until they fail--so even if you store all your family history on the computer, whether it is in a program you have purchased or an online database you have subscribed to, always keep a paper backup.

Paper Records

Download and print paper forms off the Internet, or copy them from genealogy how-to books.

Compile all your forms in a three-ring binder when you first begin your search. Organize them by name or location. Later you may add more binders, or graduate to file boxes or filing cabinets as your family history research accumulates. Consider indexing each binder to make record retrieval easier.

Fill out a Family Group Sheet for each family member and his or her immediate family. Doing this from the beginning will help you connect family members and create complete and accurate records.

Fill out a Family Tree Chart to document the names of the ancestors from whom you directly descend, and for whom you will create a Family Group Sheet. This form will help you see what you have accomplished, and who you still need to search for.

Keep a Source Summary. This is documentation of all the sources you have searched and what information you have found from each source. A separate source summary should be kept for each family tree line, so you can find information and references quickly. You may also choose to keep a Research Calendar, which is a similar record of every source you have searched and any information you have found pertaining to your ancestors.

Track correspondence relating to your genealogical research on a Correspondence Record. Use it to keep track of with whom you have corresponded, what you are writing about, and if you have received a reply or not.

Utilize a Family Tree Research Extract sheet when you are searching records or documents that can't be copied or scanned. This also works well for deeds, which are time consuming to reread.

Copy any records you want to take with you on research trips. Leave all originals at home. Carry a portable flash drive with you to save computer files on if you have access, then print the documents and add them to your binder. Also consider carrying a digital camera to photograph books and documents that cannot be photocopied, but always ask permission first.

Computer Records

There are several computer programs available online for a fee, or for free, as well as those you buy on CD-ROM and install yourself. Which program you choose depends on your computer skills, budget and organizational skills. It is certainly possible to use a free program to keep all your records, but if you become a true enthusiast of the hobby, a program that you purchase with extra bells and whistles may be more enjoyable, especially if you are considering publishing your completed research. Check online for comparisons and reviews of the year's best genealogy software.

Resources (Further Reading)

- Genealogy Today: To Organize or Be a Genealogy Slob [http://www.genealogytoday.com/columns/ruby/020612.html]
- Cyndi's List: Organizing Your Research [http://www.cyndislist.com/organize.htm]
- 2012 Best Genealogy Software comparisons and Reviews [http://genealogy-software-review.toptenreviews.com/]

BEGINNING THE SEARCH

Genealogy and searching for one's family tree is a fun and fascinating pastime. Since the United States is a relatively young country compared to many others, most of its population will have ancestors that came from other countries. For many, it is possible to trace their ancestors back centuries, allowing them to document an ancient family tree that spans numerous generations. The first step to tracing this past begins with the present.

The term ancestor usually refers to someone from whom you are directly descended. Even though you obviously descend from your parents, they are not usually referred to as your ancestors. The line begins with your grandparents and great-grandparents, and goes backwards to your 2nd great-grandparents then to your 3rd great-grandparents and so forth as far as you can trace your family tree. To begin the search you will need to locate birth information on your ancestors to keep up the search and verify you are tracing the correct branch.

Knowing how to search your family tree can provide valuable information about your ancestors. Whether you just want to learn about "where you came from", determine ethic origin, identify congenital health problems, or prove your family came over on the Mayflower, tracing the past begins with the present and goes backward.

Genealogy is the history of the descent of a person and learning where one's ancestors immigrated from is an important step in charting this process. The advent of the Internet and other forms of technology has made the process a popular hobby that can be pursued by anyone, anywhere, anytime.

Compile a list of all of your relatives that you can think of beginning with your parents and working backward, along with their birth dates, birth places, marriage dates and death dates and place of burial if they are deceased. Include their names and any nicknames and how they are related to you. If your parents are alive, verify this information, and ask for the same information on their parents. Remember to include your mother's maiden name, as this is how you will search for her ancestors to begin with. Indicate which are related to you on your mother's side, and which are related to you on your father's side as well as if they are living or deceased, and where they live, or lived. To determine your direct ancestors you will not be using all this information, but once you get started tracing your genealogy, it will come in handy.

Decide which branch of the family tree you want to trace first. It will either be your mother's side, or your father's side. Previous census records usually appear under the "male" head of household, so this may help determine your beginning point if some information is not currently available.

Ask whichever parent is from the branch you are tracing to look at the list, and make any additions or changes they can think of. Fill in any birth dates, or birthplaces and also any places of death, and any other towns and or states they may have lived in. Even an approximate date will help in your search.

Contact as many of these living relatives as possible and tell them you are working on the family tree. Ask them to provide as much information as they can, including birth dates, death dates, marriage dates and even religious affiliations on themselves and any relatives you have in common. If there is a difference in dates provided by different relatives, make a note of which relative provided the information to check later. Don't just assume one is wrong. Also ask to borrow any family records like birth and death certificates, marriage licenses, deeds and family bibles. If they hesitate to part with the originals, ask them to make copies or scan them into a computer.

Photo copy genealogy forms such as Family Group sheets and pedigree charts from books on genealogy you have purchased or borrowed from the library, or download them for free on the Internet and print them off. Family Group sheets will help you keep track of a family line or branch of the family tree.

Always document where and when you locate any information in case you need to go back and verify a piece of information. Keeping organized records from the beginning will help you trace your ancestors and make sure you are on the right track.

Look for obituaries and cemetery records to obtain and verify dates and names. Obituaries often lists names of other relatives and the decedents place of birth as well as where they are buried. Many public libraries and historical societies have access to this information either in book form, or online.

Use public Internet access at the library, or a cyber-café if you don't have your own computer. Consider purchasing a computer genealogy program to organize your research if you do have your own equipment and Internet access. Search federal census records either online or at the public library in the area where your parents and or grandparents were born, if they were born in the United States. Federal census records list the state or country where each person on the list was born.

If the town where your ancestor lived does not have an online newspaper archive, you may have to either travel to the town to view microfilm or microfiche records, typed newspaper abstracts, or even bound copies of the original newspapers to find the information, or pay a researcher to do it. Subscriptions to online genealogy databases are very helpful if you are unable to travel to your parents' or grandparents' hometown.

Some public libraries and historical societies may search for you for a donation or set fee. Search federal census records and newspaper archives online or at the library in the town where your parents and or grandparents were born if they were born in the United States. Federal census records always list the state or country where each person in the household was born and may include information such as marital status, ages of children at the time of the census, and even names of children that may have died early in childhood. Microfilm and micro-fiche are archived at many repositories and libraries.

Visit or contact the National Archives in Washington D.C., if you are searching for information on an ancestor who immigrated to America during the 1800s. Regional depositories and the Church of Latter Day Saints also have valuable records, some of which are available online.

Request the death records or certificates of any ancestors who died after immigrating to the United States. There is usually a fee and you must include specific information about why you want the record and your relationship to the deceased.

Wills and other public records may be searched if you are still missing some information.

A public record is any record in any form of media that is kept or maintained by any state, local or regionally funded agency. This includes: most court records, including liens, judgments and bankruptcies; real estate records; professional licenses; intellectual property findings; and business records such as business filings, Uniform Commercial Code documents, and public company filings. It also includes records of births, deaths, marriages and divorces.

What is or is not a public record is determined by state and federal law. What may be public record in one state is not necessarily public in a different state. Likewise, while it may be permissible to search records in a county court house for misdemeanors or felonies, the same state's criminal repository may not allow public access to the same information.

Even in this computer and Internet-based age, not all public records are accessible by computer. Many county and local records can only be retrieved by physically going to the location and manually searching through documents, recordings, microfilm or microfiche and whatever other method the records keeper or registrar uses. In some areas the term town or city clerk is applied to such a position.

In some locations, you must do the actual search yourself. In other locations it is available for a fee, and in both cases there is generally a charge for copies of any materials.

Determine when your state began keeping birth records on file. You may be able to request a copy of some ancestors' birth certificates for a fee if they were born in this country. Unfortunately, not all states began keeping records at the same time.

Check with the library, courthouse and historical society to see if any additional resources are available. Consider contacting churches to see if they have any records of christenings. Genealogy is becoming so popular; there may already be some completed family trees either online, or in some type of print form that distant relatives have completed.

Set up a separate e-mail account for correspondence pertaining to your search for birth information and other records. Post on message boards on genealogy sites for help in locating ancestors if you are having difficulty Also save a copy of any records you download to a portable flash drive so you have a back-up and an easy way to carry your genealogy records when you travel. E-mail yourself copies as well.

Resources (Further Reading)

- Free Online Family Search [http://www.familysearch.org/eng/default.asp]
- Locations of Regional Archives [http://www.archives.gov/research/arc/topics/re gions/]
- Cyndi's List of Genealogical Sites on the Internet [http://www.cyndislist.com/]

- Beginning Genealogy
  [http://www.accessgenealogy.com/beginners.htm]

DETERMINING DEATH DATES AND LOCATING OBITS

In most areas of the United States, vital records such as birth and death records were not kept until the early 1900s.

Advances in technology, and an increase in the popularity of genealogy has made finding an obituary from years or even decades ago much easier than it once was. Later records are available online in some states or through written request in others. Often a fee must accompany a written request, and in some states proof of relationship to the individual must be supplied. Whatever the case, the growing popularity of genealogy and the internet have made it easier to check someone's date of death.

Whether you choose to search a computer database, spool through a roll of microfilm or turn the pages of a newspaper abstract book, the search begins in a similar manner.

Narrow down the date of death, if possible and the place of death. Knowing an approximate date will speed up your search, especially if the newspapers have not been indexed. Knowing the exact date of death will make it even easier since you will only need to search issues within a few weeks of that date.

Most death records are available for those who have died after the late 1920s. You may request a copy of the death certificate if you are searching for someone's date of death, and you are related to him or her. These records are available from the vital records office in the state where the death occurred. You will need to provide as much information as possible, and there may be a fee depending on the state. You may also have to document your relationship, and provide a copy of your driver's license--again, depending on the state. His is sort of a double-edged sword as you are looking for a death date and they require an approximate date to even do the search.

If you have the funds to join an online database like Ancestry.com, or Archives.com (there are many more), you may be able to locate a death date. Type the name of the deceased in the search box at the online Social Security Death Index. Remember that this index did not come into effect until 1935, so the person you are searching for may not be included. If your funds are limited, check for free trials that are often available to entice customers to purchase access. Please do not just jump right in to a paid subscription without some preliminary research. You want to be sure your search is going in the right direction.

If you know where someone is buried you can search cemetery records for the approximate year of death. If you are lucky the death date and perhaps the birthdate or at least year of birth will also be available as well as names of any spouses and children.

Go to the county courthouse. Look for a copy of a will that should provide the death date you are searching for.

Make a list of names used by the deceased. Include nicknames and maiden names if the deceased was female along with any variations in spelling. Consider the fact that a wife may listed under her husband's first name. For example Betty Smith may be listed as Mrs. Henry Smith, or her name might be Elizabeth.

Check with the local library, or genealogy group to see if someone has abstracted the obituaries already. This means someone has taken the time to copy public records such as obituaries, birth announcements and marriages from the newspaper, and prepared some kind of document or book with the information that should have an index.

Check the website of the local library where the deceased lived to see if they have a link to local newspapers, or newspaper archives. Many local libraries provide access to these links to their patrons for free. Some require you to have a library card. Historical societies and genealogy sites covering the area may also provide access. Most major newspapers have not spent the time or money to abstract and post old obituaries and only host recent ones. Search any available online archives carefully. You may need to search multiple times using different name combinations. Even if you know the exact date of death, you may need to search a range of dates to find what you are looking for.

If no online resources are available ask about other genealogy resources that may contain obituaries. The format may be microfilm, microfiche or hard copy in the form of bound newspapers or newspaper abstracts. Knowing the death date comes in handy at this time if there is no index. Without at least an approximate date you would have to search day-by-day, or week-by-week depending on how often the paper is released.

Print or copy the obituary if it is allowed. Always check before assuming it is acceptable. If a source may not be copied on a copier, ask if you may take a digital photo. As a last resort, write out the obituary by hand and double-check for accuracy before you leave.

Document where and when you found the obituary if you are successful. This will be beneficial if you need to locate it again, or if you are researching you family tree.

Resources (Further Reading)

- Newspaper archives: Newspaper Archives [http://www.newspaperarchive.org/]
- Locate Death Records [http://www.vitalrec.com/deathrecords/]
- Social Security Death Index [http://search.ancestry.com/search/db.aspx?dbid=3693&cj=1&sid=ssdi_links&o_xid=0001769072&o_lid=0001769072] (requires a fee-often has free trial periods).

WHAT IS A GEDCOM?

GEDCOM, acronym for **GE**nealogical **D**ata **COM**munication, is a standard or generic database format that allows those searching for their family tree to share family history database files even if their genealogy software or operating systems are different. It was developed by the Church of Jesus Christ of Latter-day Saints' Family History Department to aid in genealogical research. GEDCOM was developed to allow an exchange data between dissimilar programs without having to manually re-enter all the genealogy data by hand. GEDCOM files contain information on families and individuals such as names, birthdates, birth locations, family ties and other genealogy data used to trace family lineage.

The information in each record is arranged in lines with corresponding numbers and tags explaining what type of information the line contains, and pointing to additional records in the file.

GEDCOM files allow those searching for family records to share records via the Internet from anywhere in the world. Most of the genealogy information in GEDCOM files can be downloaded or viewed by any genealogy software program or GEDCOM viewer.

GEDCOM files are not meant to be merged directly into a genealogy database without first being checked to make sure the files contain information on the correct people.

The GEDCOM standard was created before the popularity of multimedia. Textual data such as names and locations transfer well, but scanned images, sound clips and movies are not compatible.

GEDCOM TUTORIAL

Family records in a GEDCOM file are arranged in groups of lines that hold information about one family or FAM. Individual records are arranged in groups of lines that hold information about one individual or INDI. Each line in an individual record also has a level number. Every new record begins with the number zero to indicate it is the beginning of a new record. Each subsequent number in that record will contain a descriptive tag to explain what type of data that line contains. Tags will also point to other related information in the GEDCOM file.

Opening a GEDCOM File

The first step in downloading and opening a GEDCOM file is to establish that it is a GEDCOM file. All files in GEDCOM format should end in the file extension .ged. The only exception would be if the file is compressed into a zip format or .zip.

Once you have established that you are opening a GEDCOM file you should download it to your hard drive before opening it. It is advisable to scan for viruses on any file download, especially if the file has been sent as an e-mail attachment.

Make sure you have a backup of your original genealogy information, preferably on a thumb drive, or safely e-mailed to an online e-mail provider, in case there is a problem when you import this new GEDCOM file to your genealogy software.

Launch your genealogy software program or GEDCOM viewer. When it starts up, click the File menu option that in the top left hand corner of the screen. Select open and locate the recently downloaded GEDCOM file on your hard drive. In some genealogy software programs you will need to choose the import option to open the GEDCOM file. Make sure you save the file under a file name that is easily distinguishable from your other genealogy files before you import this information into your established genealogy database. Only when you are sure the information in the GEDCOM file is what you are looking for, follow the procedures for merging the new GEDCOM file into your existing genealogy database. This procedure may vary slightly depending on your genealogy software program, but is usually under the File option of the program. If you don't have a genealogy software program on your computer, search for free or shareware programs for GEDCOM viewers to let you open and view a GEDCOM file.

Resources (Further Reading)

- Cyndi's List: GEDCOM [http://www.cyndislist.com/GEDCOM.htm#Defin ed]
- FamilySearch.org: FAQ: GEDCOM [http://www.familysearch.org/eng/Home/FAQ/fa q_GEDCOM.asp]

HOW TO FIND WHERE YOUR ANCESTORS IMMIGRATED FROM

You already know that the term ancestor refers to someone from whom you are directly descended, and is used for relatives earlier than your grandparents, like great-grandparents, great-great grandparents and so on. Unless you have direct Native American ancestry, your ancestors immigrated to this country from another country.

Federal census records list the state or country where each person on the list was born. These records usually list where that person's mother and father were born also, if known, but only the country. You can access federal census records either online or at the public library in the area where your parents and or grandparents were born, if they were born in the United States. Many public libraries subscribe to a site called Heritage Quest where card holders may search census records for free.

Try to determine the full original name of each ancestor in your line who immigrated to America, as well as their approximate age at the time, and the approximate date they arrived in the country. Most early immigrants arrived by ship; however, prior to 1820 there were no federal laws requiring the recording of the arrival of passengers to America. This information may still be located in state and local histories, historical society records, and genealogical books and articles, but it is more time consuming and more difficult.

You search for immigration records for ancestors arriving after 1820 by checking Customs Manifests or Customs Passenger Lists. These records are available in various repositories such as the National Archives in Washington D.C., where naturalization records may also be found, the Family History Library in Salt Lake City, one of the thirteen Regional Archives (see resources for chapter 1) and in many major libraries across the country. The records for the port of New York from 1892 through 1924. have been digitized and are available online.

Resources (Further Reading)

- They Came in Ships by John P. Colletta, Ph.D.; 2002 Ancestry Publishing, Orem, Utah
- New York Port Records
  [http://www.ellisislandrecords.org]

HOW TO SEARCH FOR INDIAN/NATIVE AMERICAN ANCESTRY

Before the advent of computers and the Internet, searching for a Native American ancestor could be a daunting task. If you suspect that you have Native American ancestry, you will need to begin your search with your present family and work backward to locate the link. This is a time-consuming process, and difficult at times as there was a period in U.S. history when Indians, as they were commonly called, were not recognized as citizens and did not appear in official government records. Even when they were enumerated into the federal census, they were often listed as white. In 1860, when Indians were finally enumerated as a separate race, those not living with a tribe were simply listed as Indian, with no tribal affiliation to aid modern-day genealogists trying to search for Indian ancestors. If one of the names in your family tree may be of Indian descent, it is still possible to trace the line.

When you are searching old records, look for terms like American Indian, Indian, Native American, Cherokee, Choctaw, Chickasaw, Creek and Seminole, as well as other tribal affiliations.

If you are able to determine a possible Native American ancestor, you will next need to determine tribal affiliation. According to Ancestry.com, "The Indian Tribes of North America," written by John R. Swanton and published by the Smithsonian Institution Press, is a valuable tool with information on over 600 tribes, subtribes and bands.

Since many Indians were not listed in official records, the absence of the name of a spouse when it is evident one existed may indicate that spouse was Native American. When a Native American spouse was listed, sometimes no tribal affiliation was noted.

Tribal Affiliation

Check with the National Archives in Washington, D.C., or online for any federal and tribal census records that may be housed there. Consult the Dawes Rolls if you already know your ancestor's tribe, and where your ancestor was in 1900. This and other tribal rolls are located in repositories such as the LDS (Church of Jesus Christ of Latter-day Saints) Family History Library in Salt Lake City and other genealogical research centers or libraries.

Search tribal rolls census records, probate records, marriage records, death records and birth records for your ancestors, beginning with your grandparents and going back to your great-great grandparents if you are able. Look for terms such as Indian, American Indian, Native American and even Cherokee or other affiliation. If you find no evidence of Indian heritage by the time you reach this step, your search may be futile.

DNA Testing

Before beginning the arduous task of looking for an unnamed Native American ancestor, consider DNA testing to verify you carry genetic markers indicating Native American descent. If your haplotype does not match a haplogroup specific to one of those belonging to the Native American population, there is no blood ancestor that you are related to. Costs for this range from $150 to $400, but many individuals find it worth the price, though tribal membership will not be granted on DNA results alone.

Resources (Further Reading)

- Access Genealogy: Proving your Indian Ancestry [http://www.accessgenealogy.com/native/proving-indian-ancestry.htm]
- National Archives: Dawes Rolls Tutorial [http://www.archives.gov/genealogy/tutorial/dawes/final-rolls.html]
- Ancestry.com: Searching for your American Indian Ancestors [http://www.ancestry.com/learn/library/article.aspx?article=5601&cj=1&o_xid=0001029688&o_lid=0001029688]
- Access Genealogy: DNA-Native American [http://dna.accessgenealogy.com/dna_native_american.htm]

- ProGeneaologists:com: Native American Indian Genealogy [http://www.progenealogists.com/nativeamerican.htm]
- Native American Records and Rolls [http://www.accessgenealogy.com/native/]

HOW TO SEARCH FOR SLAVE ANCESTRY

Due to the complicated history of the birth and growth of the United States of America, many African-Americans find that they have ancestors that were slaves. Tracing these slave ancestors isn't always easy, as they were considered property, and often sold or willed, deeded and even gifted to their owner's family members. With patience and organizational skills, locating slave ancestors and determining where they came from, as well as where they went after they were freed, is an important part of tracing certain branches of your family tree.

Check Federal Census records working backwards every ten years until the 1870 federal census to locate names of your ancestors. Many freed slaves stayed in the area where they had lived as slaves. Search the records for white families in the area where you locate your slave ancestors with the same or similar surnames. These may be the slaveholding families.

Determine which of your ancestors were living in the 1860's. Just subtract ten years from their ages on the 1870 census to get this information, often census takers estimated a slave's age as birth and sales records weren't always accurate. Make a separate list of those ancestors.

Check the slave schedules for the county in which your ancestors may have lived in the 1860's. These are located at the National Archives in Washington D.C., and at some historical societies. You will be looking for the possible slaveholder name, not those of your ancestors as slaves were listed by sex, age and color only. Remember to check for variations on the spelling of surnames since records were not always accurate. Compare the ages and sexes of your ancestor's family group to those listed in the slave schedules. Keep in mind that families may have been split up between neighboring farms, but mothers and children were often kept together. Repeat this step with the 1850 slave schedule.

Determine the slaveholding family that owned your slave ancestors; begin to research that family for additional information on your ancestors that may have been included in the slaveholder's records. Look for diaries, estate and farm records and family bibles.

Document when and where you locate any information. E-mail copies of records to yourself so you always have access and duplicate records. Search online databases and join message groups for additional information, tips and support while you search for your slave ancestors.

Resources (Further Reading)

- How Do I Trace My Slave Ancestors [http://www.myslaveancestors.com/]
- 8 Steps to Tracing Slave Ancestors [http://www.familytreemagazine.com/article/Find-Slave-Ancestors]
- More Resources Available for Tracing Slave Ancestors [http://www2.tbo.com/content/2008/feb/24/ba-many-resources-available-for-tracking-slave-anc/]

- Rootsweb: Large Slaveholders of 1860 and African American Surname Matches from 1870 [http://freepages.genealogy.rootsweb.ancestry.com/~ajac/]
- Freedmensbureau.com: The Freedmen's Bureau Online [http://freedmensbureau.com/]

NOTES